Thoughts: Fruit of Experience

By

Phillippa A. Farrington

Published by Phillippa A. Farrington

Book editor: Ms. Yasmine Glinton
Cover design by Zandric Jones
Photography by Ms. Kimberley Rhaming

ISBN: 978-1-105-77244-3
Printed in the United States of America

This book is dedicated in memory of
my cousin the late poet
extraordinaire,

Nichelle Farrington

1987 - 2012

Introduction

Thoughts are the fruit of my experiences. My words are the spoken manifestation. It is my hope that the content of this book inspires you. Inspiration can drive an individual to greatness; it's on the inside of you.

5

Honesty, Forgiveness,

Harmony, Joy.

Love prevails.

6

Positive words

are

ARCHITECTURAL

7

Your life follows your

words.

What do your words

follow?

8

Happiness,

Peace,

Fulfillment,

…choice or entitlement?

9

No one can live your life
better than the original
creation

You.

10

You have purpose.

Search for it you will find it.

Know it you will pursue it.

Accept it you will fulfill it.

Greatness is innate.

Tap into it,

develop it,

share it.

Love what you do.

Be at your best.

You were born to do this.

13

The moment is when you are in the moment.

No passion,

No drive.

15

Where there is passion, there is always provision for productivity.

16

If you find yourself in an
environment where you are
unhappy, not performing at
your peak, and negatively
impacting others...

change your environment.

Change is not to be feared

but embraced.

18

Your world is only as big as your exposure to it.

19

God is everywhere

except nowhere.

20

Readiness?

Time is in God's hands.

21

Time can make you certain
about uncertainty,

but it can also make you
uncertain about certainty.

22

Position yourself to be in the right place, at the right time; all the time.

Others do not keep us prisoners of our past.

We do.

24

Previous decisions brought you here.

Present decisions will take you where you want to be.

25

The only thing worse than having sight is choosing not to see.

26

Before you commit for a life time ask yourself,

'Can I deal with this for a life time?'

27

Sometimes

that which we desire most

is detrimental.

One day you can have it all

and in an instant loose it.

Take nothing for granted.

You have been entrusted
with much.

At times you may get weary
but there is strength and
wisdom.

30

One falls with ease

but

it takes strength to stand.

Marry

experience and education.

32

Do not take experience for granted; she is an excellent teacher.

Disabilities may limit ability

but

never possibilities.

34

When education can't,

favor will!

They say bloom where you are planted, get planted.

Hating is only justified

when you are the hater.

You can convince yourself

of anything.

37

To exist simply is.

To live intentionally a choice.

To forgive a must.

Live, love, laugh, help and forgive.

Above all keep your motives pure.

40

The only truth liars speak is,
"What truth?"

The compass of the upright
is integrity.

42

When you know different;

do different.

Do not conform.

43

Exposing someone to the whole rather than segments makes them an integral part of your life.

Families should confirm public boasts of love and commitment.

Grave mistake to ignore

silence

or a loud cry.

46

There’s a message in silence.

47

The deadliest form of poison
is one without a label.

Anger bottled up is dangerous and often misdirected.

Life has balance.

If you desire joy

don’t accept unhappiness.

If your time is valuable

don’t waste it.

52

If you deserve better

don't settle for less.

If you desire success

don’t accept failure.

The foremost importance is
not that you believe in me
but that I believe in me.

About the Author

Phillippa A. Farrington is described as a young, vibrant, multitalented leader. She is an educator of ten years and has been honored as teacher of the year 2008-2010. She is always in pursuit of professional development. Miss Farrington is currently pursuing a Master's Degree from The Chicago School of Forensic Psychology.

She is actively involved in her church and community. She is Vice President of Daughters of Royalty Inc. and is committed to mentoring and counseling young females. She has also coordinated various youth programs such as the Local Government Junior Council and the Anchor Club. She has dedicated years of service to organizations such as The Pilot Club, The Anchor Club, and The Ministry of Tourism. Miss Farrington has also authored the book *For the Broken* which can be purchased on lulu.com, amazon.com or in local book stores.

www.ingramcontent.com/pod-product-compliance
Ingram Content Group UK Ltd.
Pitfield, Milton Keynes, MK11 3LW, UK
UKHW020217250726
13967UKWH00001B/39

9 781105 772443